Untold Stories

Untold Stories

Dorothy Slikker

Untold Stories
Copyright © 2019 by Dorothy Slikker. All rights reserved.

No part of this publication may be reproduced, stored in a retrieval system or transmitted in any way by any means, electronic, mechanical, photocopy, recording or otherwise without the prior permission of the author except as provided by USA copyright law.

The opinions expressed by the author are not necessarily those of URLink Print and Media.

1603 Capitol Ave., Suite 310 Cheyenne, Wyoming USA 82001
1-888-980-6523 | admin@urlinkpublishing.com

URLink Print and Media is committed to excellence in the publishing industry.

Book design copyright © 2019 by URLink Print and Media. All rights reserved.

Published in the United States of America
ISBN 978-1-64367-607-4 (Paperback)
ISBN 978-1-64367-606-7 (Digital)
01.07.19

Ruby, Charles and Dorothy Sanders

What a way to go it's so much fun trying to relive the life I led as a teenager. Where should I begin oh yes at the very beginning. My life was so different from most other kids in school. I had a father that was fun and at the same time a very strict disciplinarian. What he said goes and he advises you to remember what he says as he didn't intend to repeat it several times. He placed a curfew when we got old enough to go out with the guys; we had to be in by midnight, which was in the house not on the porch saying goodnight to our bow. If we broke our curfew it meant what daddy said no phone, or playing our records or going anywhere for six weeks, just to school and work! Unlike other kids I got to see real love develop in front of my eyes. I was about six when mama started dating (my now father) Bill Shultz. As they dated they took us on some of the dates, we got sneak peeks at the moves he always made towards my mama since she was soon to be his wife we saw lots of breast pinching. With a gleam in his eyes he would call out time for tity, we all yelled yes time for tity, as this was our signal that we were headed to the frosty stand.

Ruby, Dorothy Charles Sanders

As I watched my head would spin with images running through it wondering what it would be like to have that kind of love in my life. It was not in my world, not what I could ever expect, someone paying so much attention to just me, my daydreams kept me busy as reality set in.

Well so much for small talk let's move on. In the small town of Shafter, CA. when you started to school, the kids in your kindergarten class, would be the same kids that you graduated high school with. That's why so many of us dated guys from the nearby towns. How could you date your brother, as this was how some of our relationships progressed into being. You know how the mystery would unfold in a new relationship, it seemed as though there was nothing new to discover with our old lifelong friends. The intrigue of discovering new things and personalities was what kept the heart beating a thousand beats per minute. Thru kindergarten and grade school there would be my "boyfriend" but by the sixth and 7th grade you started to have your first crushes, all the time daydreaming they were going to be the one to lead you by the hand through your journey of life. To no avail was this ever going to happen. I remember my first big love secret was a guy from an upscale family, they had some money, or it seemed, as he always had anything he wanted. He was in the 8th grade and I in the 7th grade. We had band together he played the trumpet and I the clarinet and we both entered the music contest at the same time. Of course he won and I tried to congratulate him, this ended with him spitting in my face. I guess with all that flirting I did, it didn't make an impact the way I wanted it to go. From this I learned to let the guy make the first move.

Left to right middle row Beverly and first row Dorothy marked with an X

Well Ruby and Judy were having the opportunity to start dating so it was time to hear what to expect on dates. I was now in the eighth grade making me all of 12 years of age. Remember daddy always said I will say this once, so here we go again. He started by telling us what boys would do and say, then he gave us a demonstration how the boys were going to go about it, slipping their arms around our shoulders whispering all of the sweet nothings we wanted to hear, while doing all these things they would be trying to work their way into our panties. Daddy told us what we could allow them to get away with and closed this talk with if you get yourselves pregnant don't think you are going to give one of my grandchildren away. That always stuck in my mind as he had never adopted me and I really was not his daughter, but yet he is saying this calling it my grandchild, I guess even though he never gave me his name he gave me his heart. In my time this was not heard of staying in school and getting to graduate. Usually the more affluent families sent the girls away and after the birth they came back. It was one of the most terrible things that could happen in a small town. Finally daddy ended this talk. I know these are the things that boys will do; it hasn't been that long since I was a young whippersnapper myself. My first date was the night I graduated from the eighth grade. Mom and daddy took us to dinner and let us invite a young man. I took Gene McGraw. Last night was our 60th class reunion and who sat at our table, Gene McGraw, and after 64 years I got my good night kiss. Thanks Gene for being there and going along in such a good mood. It was a star filled night and full of magic, it didn't matter that mom and dad where there.

Dorothy and Beverly

    Showing off the dresses, which we made ourselves, and our Tony Home Permanents, all of this made it our first time to be grown up. This was the time of becoming a woman, my first pair of heels, and our first time to wear make-up, for our gift mama and daddy gave us our own personal make up kit. Our graduation from the eighth grade, I am now officially grown up and know more than my parents. A lot of things happened around this time, weather was one big thing in 1952 we had this earthquake that was just about the worst one in the State of California. It was early in the morning and it was so loud, the transformers were blowing up, it was so close to when world war 11 ended remember daddy had a brother killed, daddy came down the halls yelling my god they bombed us. It seemed like an eternity with the aftershocks, you could never relax and let your guard down. To this day this earthquake is the most talked about in our community. John tells me that his family moved outside to sleep under the trailers, everyone was afraid to return to the inside. It took a long time for the families to return to normal. Today John talks about how the quake made the cotton rows becomes so crooked that you could no longer cultivate for the weeds or run the water out to the ends of the rows. We now face the long hot summer on the farm chopping cotton, chasing the hogs and cutting the feed for the pigs. I was also present for all of the things to make our pigs a little better meat, such as removing the nuts, watching the men bite them off and applying the tar like salve. When daddy did it I was a little older and helped to hold the piglets while he applied rubber bands to the area. After about a week or two they fell off. After we finished our cotton we were farmed out to, a neighboring farmer, who needed some extra help, really bad weedy cotton. It was during the summer that we learned to drive a vehicle and tractor, so there was some excitement on the farm. On the days that were extra warm we took naps after playing in the ditch and making paths through the tulles so that daddy could go frogging at night, those frogs were always the biggest in the west and they tasted just like chicken. He never did get me to eat snake, all the time saying you have to be sporty. Daddy wanted us to learn to shoot the gun. I hated it and Beverly was a crack shot. We used to ride on the front fenders and point out the rabbits. Another thing we hunted with abundance was the coyote as they would break the watermelons and eat the heart out. Daddy used to plug them with strychnine, in other words don't try to steal the melon off of Shultz's place. One afternoon daddy came across some men stealing melons and drove up to them and asked them what they were doing? They responded with "the owner told them to help themselves as he couldn't harvest them as there was no market for them". Daddy pointed his shotgun out the window and identified himself; he took all of the money that they had on them. That was an expensive day for the thieves even if they sold them they still couldn't make a profit.

Daddy decided that we needed a better home; they discussed about building on the ranch and decided there were way too many mosquitoes, this could make us sick. He and mom financed a house and built it in Shafter, close enough so we could walk to school and town. This was in 1952; the house was the most beautiful place in the world. We all had our own space. This was actually the first time I ever had a bath in a real bathroom in a tub or even in a shower. Hot water through the pipes and I was all of 12 years old. We actually had one of those new washing machines that were in the house, but we hung the clothes on a clothesline to dry. A big yard and garden, you could not ask for more. Finally we all had our own space. They roomed Ruby and Judy together and Beverly and I, Charles had his own room.

While we were still all at home Charles had a lot of issues to deal with, being raised in a family of four girls, and a father that really had no use for him. We always ran around the house trying to get dressed all the time we would be in some mode of disrobe, not realizing the effect this was having on our little brother. Who would have ever given it a thought that this would cause feelings for him that he couldn't control. One day he called our neighbor with an obscene phone call. She recognized his voice and called the police. They kept her on the phone while they found Charles still in the phone booth. This little episode landed Charles in Juvenile for two weeks under observation. This was the first time in his life that he had boys and men around him that was not giving him a hard time. He didn't want to come home, but he had to. Daddy never did give him any space, love, or forgiveness. After a time Charles took money from mom's purse and took off to live with our blood father, Willard, who promptly put him in an orphanage. They notified mom and she sent for Charles and brought him back home. As things didn't change Charles took off again and Willard signed him into the Army at the age of 17. Well now he is with only men and did they have the wild times on leave, none of this helping Charles with his problem.

Charles later on served in Vietnam, on top of all of his problems he now has to deal with the stress syndrome of war and seeing so many of his friends die in a horrible way. He and another buddy had to plant mines in an open field, after they were finished Charles was sent into town for supplies, while he was gone they got the order to disarm the mines. His buddy was killed that day trying to disarm the mines; he had not waited for Charles to help him. I don't think Charles ever got over that one. Charles would talk about how the population of people would throw human waste at them as they got off the ship to be discharged; this was one of the most deadly wars we fought in the history of the USA. Charles was in the 101st airborne division. There were 65 brave soldiers in that division and only 12 returned home to their families. Charles passed away from cancer of the lungs due to the Agent Orange that was used in the war. He always held his head high and proud for his service to his country and he also had and endured many nights of horror in his dreams reliving the horror of war. It seemed like Charles never did have much luck with women, when he came home from Vietnam he brought a woman with him saying she was his wife. We all went to granny and grandpa's for a family gathering to honor the return of our brother and his wife; she ran off and left him the same weekend while we were at the family gathering. About a year later Charles met and married JoEd a woman with four kids and they lived on the ranch in Corcoran while Charles worked for daddy. While working on the ranch didn't work out Charles got a job in the paper factory he was about 26. On his 27th birthday he went and had drinks with some of his buddies and someone slipped him a mickie in his drink, while he was in a messed up stupor he kidnapped a girl and tried to rape her all the while he was holding her with a knife at the throat. Coming too he stopped and took her back home; he was apprehended and sent for trial. He was found guilty and put into a mental hospital until he was found to be fit enough to be sentenced. My friend's husband was an attorney and he represented and got his release as he had already served four years in the hospital.

Later he introduced us to Mary Hernandez, his new wife. I asked how they met and it turned out that Mary's brother was Charles probation officer. They went on to have two sons, Charlie Jr. and Tony. They stayed married for many years before they divorced and he married Bernice Maxine. They had met on a fishing trip, well that's all Charles loved doing so now he had a partner in life. Another thing Charles loved doing was drawing, but he didn't know how to paint. One day he came to my home in Cayucos with all the stuff you needed to do a great Bob Ross painting and said sis would you teach me how to paint. That was a wonderful afternoon Charles, I and painting.

I have now graduated grade school and was off to the adventure that was going to be the rest of my life. School, boys, registration day, the basics and my electives, this is what I thought at the time would be my world. The basics, history, math and art, art was going to be my big thing. When I got home my dad said not in my world are you taking art, what happens when you can't find a husband? Who is going to take care of you? You can't make a living drawing pictures, you will take a business course, being a secretary you can take care of yourself. During my time in the 1950's girls married and had babies. Only spinsters would be out there alone with no one loving and taking care of them. You must keep in mind that my mother had three children by the time she was seventeen years old. This put it strongly into my mind that dating was more of a game or ritual to find a husband. All the while daddy repeating you will only marry what you date.

Daddy was strict, he had to personally meet any boy we dated and give us his approval. Bob Maupin was one of these poor fellows to have to go through this ritual, he met dad and stayed for awhile for he and dad to get acquainted. After Bob left I was so excited saying is he ok, huh? Daddy said no and now I was faced to tell him no date, with egg on my face. Ruby later asked to go out with Bob and dad let her go, why???? Daddy said he was too mature for me and that was the end of that.

I asked John what it was about me that made him want to date me. I guess it was because you were a country girl, not a city girl. Maybe that was what my dad felt about me, I was too country and could fall prey for a city boy, you know about me being so simple and being taken advantage of before I could make the right decisions about the direction I wanted my life to move forward. Ruby being older and with a little more experience about boys lead my dad to let her have a little more leeway with the fellows at school. Ruby was beautiful and had absolutely no trouble in the boys dept. She had many of them after her.

Judy was not far behind being the beauty that she was. Long thick reddish brown hair and a slim body she had a lot of guys after her all the time. Judy found her guy from the neighboring town of Wasco that was where Ron was from. They eventually ran away and got married. I guess we all had the drive for marriage as that what it was that we were reminded about. Don't be a spinster that has a lot of drag to the life left to live. It was during Judy's senior year of high school that she went through the bedroom window and took off with Ronald Scoggins. They married a short time later and had three children Ronald Joe, Janice and Carlene. Judy always had the dream of becoming an airline stewardess; she was 1/2 inch too short. Later after about 10 years Judy and Ron divorced and she made a living for herself and children working as a waitress. She was one of the best waitresses I ever saw, it was amazing how she could work a table and be able to support three children on tips alone. Judy went on to marry two more times at the end of her life she was living with a boyfriend in

Ruby Sanders

Judy Shultz

These are my two older sisters Ruby and Judy, Judy is seven days older than Ruby and they are 18 months older than Beverly and I, of course, Beverly is three months older than me, and we are 22 months older than our brother Charles.

Charles Sanders

Beverly Shultz   **Dorothy Sanders**

This was like having two sets of twins in high school at the same time. You know this had to be an expensive adventure for any father, let alone doing it for kids that were not his own. You have now met the Shultz family that was thrown together for life when I was eight years old. Beverly and I are the only ones left on this earth from a family of five siblings. Through thick and thin we all stuck together even though we had our differences and arguments throughout our lives.

My freshman year there were these two boys, Donnie Thompson and Oscar Little, I thought they were the neatest things alive. I guess I ran after them a little too hard, enough so they dodged me for the next four years. About in the middle of my freshman year I met Choyce Jackson, he was what everyone wanted, and he was bad to the core. Leather jacket, dark hair combed into a v onto his forehead. Most of all, this guy liked me. He looked the James Dean part, he should have had his own motorcycle or sports car, but we always had to double date. He liked to dance and I was one to never miss a school dance. I guess you might say he was a little rough around the edges; he loved to kiss and make out (like daddy said they would) so in my mind he was a keeper. Choyce had a good friend Gary Bromwell, Gary had a thing for Ruby and Ruby thought he was god's gift to the world. Even before Ruby died at the age of 65 yrs. Ruby said I sure miss my true love Gary. Ruby and Gary ran away to get married, his family was fit to be tied as they thought Ruby was not good enough for Gary and our parents felt the same way about Gary. Gary's parents reported their car stolen and Ruby and Gary were picked up in Yuma, Az. They were put in jail until their parents got there to pick them up. Ultimately they were forbidden to see each other anymore. Well you know how that works; one night daddy was checking us when he got up for the bathroom. He found Ruby and Gary naked in the back yard getting it on in the light of the moon. Daddy ran

Gary off and almost killed Ruby, the Dr. said one more blow to the head and she could have died. Gary's parents signed Gary into the army and Gary was ultimately killed in a jeep crash while he was in the service.

Choyce was noted by the school counselor as undesirable. The counselor was a friend of daddy's and she notified him to not let me date him as he was always in trouble. At this point daddy started the vigil of sticking to his guns and not letting Choyce come to the house. After awhile Choyce quit coming around or calling me. I thought well there goes another one. I did not know that daddy threatened to kill him if he didn't stop seeing me.

George Abshure was a fellow that was cute and a year older than I. We dated for awhile. He was another one to dump me, god I am having no luck with my relationships. I always had a thing for Ed Parks, he liked me to (so he said) he told me he couldn't date me because he couldn't look me in the eyes. He thought I had bedroom eyes. Another fellow Jack wanted to date me but I considered him too tall. Jack was 6' 3", much too tall for me.

Across the field from our home in town they built a horse racing track. Well they brought the horse trainers from back east. One kid (his father trained horses) was Bill Valendingham, blonde; blue eyed and the world's best dancer. Again, not from Shafter, so every girl in the school was after him. Then there was Max Spencer, it seemed that I was going to be that spinster secretary after all. Can you believe that on Graduation Night I Dorothy Sanders didn't have a date? Well its true no date, no future as far as I could tell.

Beverly and John Sivils

Beverly had her share of fellows also, but with Beverly her relationships always took off into the world of serious love. I always liked to try to get in the way of them, jealousy I guess. Beverly was in love with Jim Thornsberry and they were engaged, he always kept coming on to me and I guess she caught us and broke off her engagement with him, I didn't want him either, Jim wound up marring a school friend of ours, in the long run she met and fell madly in love with John Sivils. This is their wedding picture; they had three children and three grandchildren and were married in 1959 until John's death in 2008. A long union this was to be and a beautiful family for the Sivils family. We did a lot of things alike, such as our art. Beverly is one fantastic artist, before her stroke she could have been a national sensation. After the stroke Beverly started painting again and gained a lot of her passion back for awhile, even teaching students in her nursing home. After a few years she has seemed to have lost the desire to continuing painting. Unlike me

Beverly had this great ability to draw, almost anything she saw, I took photographs and traced what I had seen. Either way the paintings from both methods could be considered a masterpiece. Beverly had the desire to hang on to everything she painted and when she gave one away, it was not beneath her to ask for it back, almost like she had loaned it to you. On the other hand I wanted to sell my work, it made me feel good to know someone would pay me for my art, I always hoped they liked it in the long run and would enjoy it for many years to come.

We used to have lots of home parties and they were well attended by our friends, because mom and dad would be there, they always served beer and mom liked to dance with the boys. This helped to make us more popular with our friends as they liked mom and dad.

During the summer I met Harry Franativich, he was in the Navy and on leave visiting friends in Shafter, by the time summer was over he left and went back to the ship and shipped out. We tried a long distance relationship, but to no avail. I had a best friend, Vernice Tabor, which was supposed to attend one of our parties one night. She backed out and went with her brother and his navy buddies, they were drinking heavy and in the fog they ran their car under a cotton trailer it killed them all. For Veronica's family it was a tragedy as they lost all of their family in one night. This accident was such newsworthy article that they hauled the car from school to school to try and get the kids motivated to quit drinking. That was so long ago 62 years since I was a lowly freshman at Shafter High.

Now comes time for School to start and it would be my first year at Bakersfield College, I really didn't want to go to college the day that I was supposed to register, we got off of the bus to early and had to walk about four miles to the college, along the way we came across the marine recruiting office, we went in and all took the test for enrollment and we all passed, Me, Beverly and Cathy Kendrick. We were not old enough we had to be 18, but if our parents would sign for us then they would take us. Daddy said to go to school for one year and if I still wanted to he would sign the papers.

I dated Louis Wolf, it went nowhere. In school I carried a full load and held down two part time jobs. I majored in Child Psychology, by this time I was afraid to attempt art so I didn't venture into that direction. I had a lot of child development classes and Home Ec. Classes. I carried a full load with all of the required classes.

I joined the Home Ec. Club, and the Flag Twirlers with the band. All through High School I played in the band and now I wanted some of the glamour marching behind the band.Our Home Ec.

Club joined forces with the Ag. Club in the year of 1958 to build a float for the Home Coming Game, being a farmer's daughter I had access to a cotton trailer to build said float. When I got the trailer there, one was already there just slightly larger than the one I brought. A farm boy by the name of John Slikker had pulled their cotton trailer and they decided to use the bigger one. As the night progressed I had a friend Carol Cunningham, we decided he would be just right for her. John kept coming around me and struck up a conversation by saying I bet my car horn is louder than yours, of course I being the competitive one took him up on his bet. My car was a 1949 Chevy Convertible and it had a very loud horn. John being a gentleman let me blow mine first, when he blew his horn everyone died laughing as they all knew that John had mounted a truck horn in his trunk of the car. We got John to take Carol home that night, the next day at school, she told me that she would never date someone I picked for her. I asked her why? Because all he did was ask about you that made me feel really good. All the things I never wanted in my life a tall farm boy.

The following week we met at the house again and finished the float for the parade. I had two friends there and I knew John had a crush on Betty Wooley because he asked me a lot about her. We had been working on the float for about three weeks at this time. I couldn't ride with John because of marching with the band. He came up to me and asked if I cared if he asked Betty and Lacretia to ride with him in the parade. My answer was (remember we had never dated at this point) no, but if you do, don't ever ask me out. What an ultimatum I gave him! He pulled the float with his 1957 Chevy all alone that night and later came up and said would you like to go for something to eat after the game? Yes I would and that night we started going steady. People say and wonder do you believe in love at first sight? Yes I do and it was the same for my oldest son Jon.

Now I had to get my trailer back to Shafter, I guess my teacher asked John's professor to see if John would do this chore for me. John Olglesby was his professor, this allowed him to lay claim to the fact that he got us together. John volunteered, but stating the girl that brought it has to go with him as he delivers it back to her Uncle's place. This took place before our first date, I asked my mother to have snacks prepared for us and I would bring him over for them to meet. They weren't home, that was what one should expect from my parents.

Dorothy Sanders 17 yrs. and John Slikker 18 yrs this was in the first year that we met and the picture were taken in my granny's home. John seemed to fit right in with my family, he didn't show that he thought he was out of his social class and he never acted like he was ashamed. Here was someone taking me for who I was, not what I was, god bless this fellow. Now remember my father's words about being a young whippersnapper himself? Well here is the younger version of a whippersnapper all hands and arms even throwing in a few legs with all the sweet talk, he's a keeper, he loved to kiss and make out making all the sensations come to a new high and then oh our first time, who could have known it was like this. Here he was all the things I didn't want to spend the rest of my life with, tall and a FARMER. As the year progressed, we did everything we knew to get to know more about each other. John liked to fish, I didn't, but I went anyway and carried his catch and watched as I sat on the rocks along the Kern River. Sometimes we would stop at the Hot Springs and mess around in the pool. What I wouldn't do or try for this guy, after the first time, we always made love. I was lucky that I did not get pregnant. Every day John would say I can't wait until you are my wife.

One day John picked me up at the drive in where I was working and we went to the school carnival, he said let's get married. He bought the license and we got married at the school carnival using a chicken leg band for a ring. That was our first wedding. John had to have loved me as he had to drive 45 miles in one direction to pick me up and then we would go back to Bakersfield for dinner and a movie, ending with us going to the farm to change his water in the fields, then driving back to Shafter, where we parked for a while just to spend more and more time together. John then had to drive back to Bakersfield. It makes for a long day and a lot of dedication. One of our dates, remember it's in the 1950's, we went fishing on the Kern River and had a picnic, came back to his parents home and cleaned up and then went to the movies or drive-in (known as the passion pit). We fell asleep and didn't wake up until 3:00am. (C U R F E W WAS 12:00pm) remember go nowhere for 6 weeks! Boy was I in trouble just like the Everly Brothers song Wake up Little Susie. I was still 30 min. away from home; you should have heard the excuses I was making up. Finally John said let me handle it, I'm sure your dad had things happen to him too. OK. You don't know my dad there are no excuses. When we got home there was Daddy at the door waiting for us to come up with the story. Come in and explain yourselves, you know the rules. Then he surprised us with Dorothy you are old enough so I am lifting your curfew, John is a responsible young man. We like him and want him to keep coming around. Little did they know how he was, kept running around in my mind. There were lots of dates that consisted of changing John's water and then driving to Wasco to our farm to change the water at our ranch, then John driving back to Bakersfield. On one of these dates John helped me shovel gyp into the agitator; it fed the gyp into the ditch for treating the alkali that was prominent in the desert soil. Marginal soil was about all daddy could afford.

During John's high school days he was active in the Agricultural program and active in Future Farmers. He even made the State Farmer in his Senior Year. This is about the highest degree you can make in the Future Farmers of America. John was always diligent in learning to do things in the right way and he had a father that made sure John would and could participate in all of the programs that were available to him.

John Slikker

John Slikker Jr.

John was a good student throughout his school years and this has carried him on through life, marriage, family and being one of the top 60 farmers in the United States. John has always taken great pride in himself and family.

John welding for a completion in High School

John made California State Farmer one of the highest honors in the Future Farmers of America. When he showed his prize winning Black Angus he and a friend of his always vowed for the Grand Champion and the reserve Grand Champion, one of the prizes was a considerable amount of money and getting to pick out his project steer from an Angus Breeder, John Hersey from Oildale, Ca. The following year with his prize Angus John again placed high in the Angus Show earning a good sum of money for his efforts. The value of the steer was the price per lb. paid by some of the businesses in town. Johns steer weighed in at 1,000 lbs. and John was paid 65 cents per lb. J.C. Penny was the business that made the purchase. As he entered Bakersfield College he changed into more of the field crops as he put in more and more hours on the farm. John was learning from his father and when his father retired John took over all of the business.

Now with all that I have shown you could you not fall in love with this tall farmer. I couldn't. John's dad bought the farm from Fred Kampe John's mom's uncle. It was a two year lease with the option to buy in 1948, and then purchased it in 1950. He purchased the land at $200.00 per acre. John lived on Quantico Ave about 5 miles away from the farm. It became a fixture to see this young boy peddling his bike down the Edison Highway to help his dad with the chores in farming. This he learned from a young age the same way that I had done on our farm. As you can see from the pictures provided John learned a lot of skills to further help him throughout his life. With his free time John liked to build model airplanes and fly them. I asked him what he would have liked to have been if he had not been in farming and his reply was a train engineer, or Truck Driver. He always needed to be outdoors or working with his hands. He never would have been happy in any office surroundings. I think some of his happiest times in High School were in the Future Farmers.

Farmers. They seemed to be busy with their projects, mostly raising his black angus. Even as an adult he loves telling the story about him and some of the guys riding the freight train with their steers to the California State Fair. All of the things they did, jumping along the top of the train carrying their milk buckets and throwing milk on the kids in the next car, and one time when Lawson Bartell got off the train and ordered hamburgers for all of them and the train started to leave Lawson running yelling cancel that order after all he had a train to catch. As they pulled out of the station the Ag teacher telling them to stay inside with the steers this they promised just like the teenagers of today.

John is the second one from the left

This is the lineup of the pen of five champion steers. John always took top honors in any of his projects. This is the way he was taught to lead the vision of doing only his best at all things he set out to do in his life. Some of these guys remained good friends throughout their lives.

Mama and Daddy kept telling me that if I didn't straighten up my attitude that John wouldn't keep coming around, I answered I don't care if he doesn't. One time we went to a party that the Farm Club had and they were making homemade ice cream and I sat on the machine while they churned it, they kept flirting with me and I back at them, John was so mad that he took me right home. Mom and dad started in on my back side that he wasn't going to come back. So what was my reply? It's funny how our relationship was so solid that we could weather any storm. Through our first year we dated and helped each other and found in discovery how much our backgrounds were alike. I knew that a farmer never had a steady paycheck only at the end of a harvest. I thought I knew everything about becoming a farmer's wife; oh boy did I have a lot to learn. John's dad made it easier for us by paying John $400.00 per month; I learned to plan meals by using the recipes for the dishes I had planned to prepare during each week. With this dedication to watching our money, I was able to pay all of our bills and keep good healthy meals on the table; we were able to save $100.00 each and every month. I knew in my heart that if things got real tough I could fall back on my background and make it happen to the good for both of us.

One year later the two clubs got together again to build another float, after John picked me up and as we were going on the freeway John pulled the car over to the side of the road and he formally proposed to me with a real diamond ring. I cried and said yes with all my heart' I did not know that he had already asked my dad for permission to marry me, then we proceeded to the float building party and let all of our friends know about our plans. The fowling April we got married.

Curfews were strict in the town of Shafter; you couldn't be out after 10:pm, if you were caught out and you were not 18 yrs. old they would haul your pretty butt into town and call your parents. To let you know John and I were parked on the canal bank in Shafter, after we finished our love session, John opened the door of the car to straighten his clothes and I mine, what did he see? Two boots and as he looked up all he could see was a badge, the officer said zip up your pants boy and show me some identification, John did as he was told and I had to do the same, saved by a birthday, this was my 18th birthday and I was still on time for my daddy's curfew time table of 12:00 midnight. This was during the crime spree of people coming up on couples without lights, watching them; they would then open the car doors and order the girl out at gunpoint and raping her and killing them both. That was all we could think about when we discovered the boots, just how long had this officer been at the side of the car? We felt lucky to be able to get to the comfort of home and parents. Also one of our favorite places to park was in my cousins grape field. Ken Schultz informed me at the 60th class reunion last night that the grape vineyard was now gone and is a new car lot. So many things change.

Next came Thanksgiving and Christmas, we had to make the choice of which one do we attend. I had never been away from home on Christmas and it was a special time for the Shultz family, John conceded that we would spend Christmas with my family this year and Thanksgiving with his family. From then on every year we would turn it around. This was all before we married and it went good enough that we kept to the ritual even after we got married. Our time was filled with school, dating and planning our wedding. We even found and rented our house for after the wedding. We proceeded to acquire furniture; which was given to us by the families. This we appreciated as our little love nest began to grow. Now we didn't have to find a place to park, like the grape vineyards, and canal bank. One of the funniest things to happen to us was we had a car wreck while looking for a room to spend our wedding night, duh we had our love nest. What could we have been thinking?

Easter Break; our wedding, a week away from school doing what we wanted with our time and each other as we were now an old married couple on our Honey moon. There were a lot of things to do for getting ready for the big day. Shopping for a wedding dress, clothes for the honeymoon, flowers for the church, the wedding cake, wedding pictures, everything went as planned except for the big day. We invited around 300 people and had in attendance around 250. We included relatives on both sides and our friends.

I had to get my Maid of Honor and Bridesmaids and flower girl. I must include my guest book attendants and find a time slot for my two cousins to play music at the reception. Yes there had to be someone to sing at the ceremony, the minister Reverend Krug. Is this all that must be done? Oh no I forgot the flower's were to be delivered and John had a busy day also. The worse thing was the church was in a different town and the family took all the cars to work at the church. HELP!!! I can't get to my hair appointment. Lucky Beverly came to the house and she saved the day by doing my hair for me, getting it combed right before it was time to go down the aisle, Beverly came through again. I trusted her with helping me as she was a licensed beautician. I should have chosen her for this in the first place. I did finally make it to the church in Wasco. All was beautiful and I was now MRS. JOHN W. SLIKKER JR. what more was there to life? It would be to my awaking what was to appear in the future. I actually had the gall to think that John's family would love and except me into their family as mine had of John, they truly did love him as a son. After all John was a farmer.

Mr. & Mrs. John W. Slikker Jr.

Here we are getting ready for the rest of our life. Armed with our love and respect for each other on April 9th 1960 we became man and wife for better or worse.

We took the week and jaunted to Las Vegas for a few days and visited some of the sites I was too young to gamble so I was scared to death. We took time to cross over Death Valley, but in doing so we had to go through this small town of Pahrump, way out in nowhere, there was just a small service station and one casino to be found. John was having trouble with his water hose on the car and they fixed it at the moment, they didn't have the right kind of hose, but they made do. Charging John $12.00, at the time that was a lot of money, we went on our way with John grumbling he was never coming back to that town anymore. Here we are today retired in Pahrump, NV.

As we crossed Death Valley it was late and getting dark and we had no reservations for the night, the restaurants were closed, in a small town they close the doors early. We found a room with a little kitchen in Lone Pine; here I fixed our first meal as Mrs. Slikker. Everything was perfect as we traveled up to Reno, here we spent a couple of nights and then on to Lake Tahoe. Oh so romantic nothing could be better, from Lake Tahoe on to our new home in Bakersfield, Ca. Monday morning here we go back to the same old grind, school, we had some classes together. Let's take math, the subject I detested but to no avail John will help me, we do our homework together and he WILL HELP ME "wrong" he informs me that I must do it myself or I will never learn anything, let's wait for English and see what I tell him when he needs help in this class, YOU MUST DO IT YOURSELF OR YOU WON'T LEARN ANYTHING. The old saying what goes around comes around.

Graduation night was really dramatic as I wanted to graduate as Dorothy Slikker, they said no as I went through school as Sanders to make a long story short the three of us graduated. Yes we were expecting our first baby.

Our little love nest was not in the best part of town and the neighbors were always fighting. One night the young man shot at his grandmother's house and we decided it was time to find another place to live. We looked high and low for apartments, or houses, when the landowners' saw my belly they decided they didn't want a young mother and child as they had the reputation of letting things go.

John had saved enough money that he could have bought a house so he talked it over with his dad. Dad said John if you would move into the old cement block house for awhile I will build you a house here on the ranch. So that was what we did. We moved into the block house with a dirt road to the main road. We had no telephone and when it rained you couldn't get out. Christmas was coming on and we had done our Thanksgiving dinner with no trouble using the road. It was now time for the Christmas Parade in town, I had just gone to the Dr. that day for my check-up and the Dr. told me that I still had a few more weeks before delivery. Taking the information in hand we headed out for the parade and came right home and had a snack now it's time for bed. When I raised my leg to get into bed I peed all over myself or so I thought. Now some slight pain and red discharge was visible and I told John we need to go to his mom's house and call the Dr. It had rained and the dirt road was a mess, but we made it to his mom's house, John asked to use the phone; she told him no go on to the hospital and they will call the Dr. from there. Within four hours our little bundle of Joy had arrived. We named him Jon Edwin Slikker.

This cement block house was built by John and his father for the man who worked on the farm, in 1952 we had a big earthquake it scared this fellow so bad, I think they said his name was Frank, he left and went back to Oklahoma, they had tornado's there but at least you could see them coming. To this date he never came back. When we moved into this house it was overrun by rats, I mean big rats. When you pulled the car into the cover at night with the headlights you could see them jumping everywhere. At night you could hear them running across the floor, John's grandpa gave us a couple of cats and in no time at all they had them all gone. During the night you could hear the cats chasing them and sliding across the floor and hitting the walls, with the loudest bang. The month of February of 1961 we moved into our new home with all of the modern convinces of the time. My new home was more that anyone could ask for. I had taken interior decorating for an elective in College and I proceeded in using my interior design knowledge to furbish our new home. No one informed me in class that the best was not always the best way to go. Children and pets on an expensive wool carpet were not going to work, as I soon discovered. By this time life has hit me right in the face, here I had to do all the work alone, where all my life I had some help in the form of sisters, lucky for me that I had all of the newest products of our time at my disposal to help me out. Also, little did I know that the grass is always greener on the other side. Life is as life is.

Life on the farm kept John and I busy especially since we started our family right away. Trying to keep the romance alive was hard to do when you are chasing little ones all day, but while the kids were little I would feed them first and change into my fancy floor length gown and robe and greet him at the door with a big smile, he would grin all through his dinner. John was the type of man who loved having his woman be sexy at all times in the evening, he informed me that he wanted me to wear a garter belt and nylons to bed otherwise I wasn't sexy to him. I wanted to tell him the same things about him to make him manlier for me, but did I want to make him feel small, I don't think so, John was a man who liked all of the soft fabrics that a woman had a choice to wear. Make up was a big thing too. I did my best but it was hard among the dirty diapers, food on the floor, oh my god it's time to start dinner, how do I get the kids calmed down enough so that their father could relax after a hard day in the fields. It was a good thing that our house was there, he could then come in and take a break and cool off. It was not long after Jon was born that I found out that we are expecting baby # 2. Nothing went right with this pregnancy and in the 7th month we lost the baby. It had died in the early stages and I carried it into the 7th month. The Dr. asked if I wanted to know the sex and I declined as I don't think I could have lived through it if I had lost my only little girl, so we never knew. I decided that since we had one child we might as well finish out our family in the early stages of marriage, so that by the time they were older we would still be young and would have all the fun of growing up with our kids, and boy did we make the most of it.

As soon as the Dr. said it was safe to try again we got pregnant with our second son. During the pregnancy I had a lot of trouble. We had a close call (wreck) on the freeway, I told John that by the time we got home I would need to go to the hospital, and sure enough that is what happened. The Dr. had to give me shots to stop the birth and then he later, as the baby went so far overdue, he had to give me shots to make him enter this world. Next comes naming this fine healthy baby boy. It took filling out 3 different birth certificates to finally get John to say I want to name him Jake William Slikker. Little did he know this is one child that would give him his most challenging moments of being a father, as Jake grew older he would never fit into the main road stream of life? Jake loved music and when he was in High School and grade school he was always in music, playing the sax. During High School we let him take organ lessons. The teacher would play the song and Jake would take from there, never learning to read music. We got him his first guitar and he was on his way. When he was in his junior year of school, the teacher wanted the students to discuss what they wanted to be when they grew up. Jake said would you like one of my cards? He had started his own hay hauling business, developed his own logo "You Call We Haul". On his off season he would work for spreading co. spreading manure and seeding fields, also working as a mechanic repairing tractors and trucks. This boy could do almost anything with his hands. At night he so enjoyed playing in bands at the bars. This is where he started his drinking and doing drugs as this was the scene he placed himself into. Jake later married three times and fathered three sons, Jake Jr., Tyler and William. Tyler is in college to become a probation officer, William is a musician, Jake Jr. passed on in the first few months of his life of Crib Death.

Here comes the last one of the bunch, another boy whom I got to name, I had always wanted a son named David Wayne, so I promptly place his title upon him. He was the cutest little thing, his hair was so white and he had the darkest brown eyes. We noticed that he would do some wheezing during the night, the Dr. said he had allergies, so not to worry, he was perfect. Being the youngest he never had to do things for himself, if one of his big brothers didn't do it for him, mama did. David loved to wear hats, when he couldn't find one he wore a Tupperware bowl for one. One of the best places for these boys to play in their sandbox and they didn't like sand in their clothes so off they came. There they were pushing their tractors and trucks, making all the proper sounds with their bare bottoms shining to the world and everybody. We used to flood the lawns and that was when they got to play in the water and boy did they love their water slide, it was a slip and slide, cool way to play on our hot summer days. It was about the time David was four I started having my fill of babies and wanted to have something else a little more glamorous to do with my life and time. John bowled and belonged to the Elks Club and I wanted something else to do also. Every time I brought up the subject John would say wait until the kids are older. I felt like I had a rope tied to my neck. One time I wanted to join the Emblem Club, and or the Junior Women's Club he would say wait and before he could finish I felt the rope being tightened even tighter. The kids started getting older and John working harder and longer hours I felt as though I was in this all alone. One time when we were having an argument John said I need to go to work, he always used this excuse as going outside he was at work. I shouted if you go through that door I will not be here when you get back. John yelling back if you are not here, you are not coming back. I yelled when I leave I am going out as I came into this marriage with nothing and furthermore you are keeping the kids. It was at that moment that I realized why the house was built on the farm. It was an asset that I could not lay claim, it dawned on me that I really had no home. I told John I have no home for the kids and you do and you have made me into a dependent woman, I did not like that feeling. I am going out of this marriage just as I came into it with nothing. I will see the kids any time that I want to. John didn't go to work and we stopped and cooled down. Today we laugh that neither of us wanted the kids. This has been the only big fight that we have had to endure up to this point. John conceded and told me to find a job and work if that would make me happy. Now what could I do as all I had ever done was work in the fields. We had a friend whose mom owned a dress shop, I talked to her and she needed a partner for financial support so I bought into the shop in 1969 for the sum of $1,500.00 in turn she was going to teach me all about the business, buying inventory and such. We also agreed that all the proceeds would be reinvested into the shop to build the inventory and refresh the look of the business. After a couple of months Betty started complaining that she couldn't make it at home because Frank her husband didn't make enough at the cleaners where he worked, I gave in and she started drawing money monthly and mine stayed in the business, again a few months later she needed even more money from the business. The business wasn't making that kind of money so I told her she could buy me out and she couldn't so I told her she had to go as she was milking the business dry. Now here I was I had to sink or swim.

Now what was I going to do to make the shop different than any other shop in town. What could I offer? Yes service, I was a very good seamstress so I decided to give free alterations with your purchase and I could also fit you for the alterations. Now what else, make the husband comfortable while his lady shopped, I put in a couple of chairs and a small table and served coffee. Also I joined the American Women's Business Association. I also changed the look of the merchandise to reflect the look for the business women. This association used me for fundraising fashion shows, Ann Gutcher; from the Ann Gutcher show invited me on her show to do a fashion show. Later on, especially in the winter months she would call at the last minute to have me fill in when her show got snowed in coming over the mountain. I had shop models and could pull clothing for them and have them meet me at the studio and we took over with the program, showing clothes and talking about the latest fashions.

I guess I was fairly good at this as I was asked if I would like to have my own show about fashions. I was flattered and agreed to do this it lasted for a couple of years, they would bring the crew to my home and the models would stay for soup and sandwiches, this venture gave me a lot more attention in the community and soon I was doing a show a week for different organizations in the city of Bakersfield. I was doing a fashion show at the Holiday Inn and the Harlem GlobeTrotters were there, they all came up to me and introduced themselves to me. I guess I did a good job.

A lot of my shows included a man's store and children's shop. Being a family and getting involved with helping each other John and my sons all did their share of modeling, even with John buying some of the things he modeled.

At one of my Christmas shows my Santa Clause pulled a no show and I was desperate for a Santa. Since my home was where it was being filmed and John was out in the field,

"SANTA" I sent one of the kids out to get their daddy and he played Santa in the show. As the models would come down the hall, John would say come to Santa, he would have them sit on his lap and say and what would you like to have for Christmas little one. The model would stand up and I would talk about giving her the outfit she was modeling and then talk about the fabric and the co. that manufactured the outfit. Again John saved the day for me. He was getting involved in the things I liked to do.

Dorothy commentating a fashion show

When I got well acquainted with these working women I got involved with their lives. Some became some of my dearest friends. I told you about the coffee for the husbands, well I soon learned that if I got to work early I received phone calls to see if I had the coffee on yet, if so they would come and have their morning coffee before work and pick out things they would like to try on. After they left work they came and finished their shopping and I the fitting, I took the clothes home and did the alterations. Early to work and late to leave, this was the notch that I carved out for myself. First of all if you wanted a job at Slikker's, you had to know how to sew. Later after retirement I did alterations for the shops in the town that we lived in. Some of my regulars would continue to call me and I would go to their homes and fit the outfit and take it home to do the alterations. After I sold my shop I had people wanting me to work for them, Shoe Tree and Things wanted me to be a buyer for their shop, I did it for awhile until she started having me doing the alterations for her shop two. I wanted to start slowing down. After all John and I had purchased a place in Bodfish and we would like to spend some of our time there. We had gone up and picked out a place and went home to buy a mobile home for the lot. As John, being one of the biggest procrastinators in the world. When I got to the mobile home lot John was sitting on the steps and he said should we be doing this? I said hell no since we have gone into debt for the lot and taken out a loan for the home. I guess we sit and quit now. It was a godsend as it became home to us during the worst dust storm in Kern Co. People were killed that were caught out in the dust storm; it was so thick you could not breathe. On the ranch we had lost power so there was no water or air conditioning. So much soil had been moved by the wind that all of the canals and ditches were filled; it reminded me of the stories my granny used to tell us about the dust bowl in the thirties.

After I left Shoe Tree and Things I worked at Bakersfield College in the office for awhile and along with the board and John Brock we fashioned a Fashion Merchandising Dept. and later I went to help a friend of mine in her shop doing just the things she needed done, alterations was one of the many things I fell into doing, you know the things I was known for. Her daughter was an artist, Lois Fox. Lois kept telling me to come to the gallery and take her lessons. I kept putting her off as it had been so long since I had painted anything.

She just kept after me and I told John and he finally said why don't you go take those lessons? I did and from that day in 1976 my brush has been in my hand at all times. I kept doing the things that made me want to paint along with the best of them.

Figure 1 Reba Mc Entire

Art in my life was a scary thing for me to pursue as I had been denied for so many years to pursue this venue, did I still have enough drive to accomplish this feat? Remembering my grannies saying if you don't put your foot out there you can't ever get it chopped off. Thus you will never experience the thrill of your first painting, even if at first you don't succeed keep a sucking till you do succeed. Oh these sayings are so good to live by even if they sound so crude. I took John's advice and signed up for classes. Our first lesson I painted a tree in dark brown and then we used turpentine on our brushes and proceeded to wipe off some of the dark brown to make a lighter bark. Later we added a river or stream some grass and a fence. I thought it was a masterpiece.

This is the painting I always teach my students first

The painting I have just shown you is the first painting that I would have you paint, it teaches you how to do trees, shows depth perception, I also explained about direct and indirect lighting. I explain how to do the fence so that it looks like it recedes. Unlike when I first took lessons I had 8 lessons before my teacher did a black and white so that I could understand what was going on. Her method of teaching I call monkey see monkey do.

My house in the fog was one of my first paintings and I hated it, it bugged me for quite a few years and then I tried to make an improvement by adding a tree and that didn't help it either. As I continued to study under Lois I became friends with the owner of the gallery, Mrs. Mize. Lila did a lot of china painting and it inspired me enough I told her I wanted to paint my own dinnerware service. Dorothy you are not a good enough artist to accomplish this feat. You must be much more precise to paint a china set of dishes. Your work has to be more consistent throughout the theme you have chosen and your work seems to be different with each painting you do. After Lois left the gallery I continued to paint with Naomi Mize under her I learned even more techniques at least enough to venture out on my own. Every once in awhile they would have an artist that was a little more well known in the art field and I would work under him on a two day seminar. With this feat I felt more comfortable about being able to follow a complete stranger's instruction and turn out some very nice work on my own. As any beginner a teacher has to instill the confidence in a student that they do have the ability to improve with practice. They tried to tell me that I had to pick a venue to become known for, I found this to be boring and felt I had to paint what it was that made me want to keep painting. Each new painting was to become a new challenge for me and this is what kept my attention in facing that blank canvas, turning me on one might say. I needed the challenge and the self satisfaction of completing that project. Oh yes granny, setting a goal and completing it. That's the motivation for me; my granny is sitting on my shoulder all the time.

Well now I had a lot of things going on in my life, dress shop, painting, fashion shows and TV show about fashions. How did I balance all of this it was with the help and support of John Slikker, he took over the care of the two older boys and took them to the field with him daily after they got home from school and I had David, the youngest, in Nursery School. One day when I was preparing for my first at home fashion show, I rushed home and started preparing dinner as I had to get right back to town, load the show in the car and meet the models at the home. While I was preparing dinner the phone rang, Mrs. Slikker isn't someone picking up David? Oh no!! I forgot David at school, I rushed back to town, eight miles away, rushed home and barley made it on time for the show. Today over 40 years later David has not forgotten that his mother forgot him; I can still see him standing there with his teacher crying.

After I sold the shop and helped my friends in their shops, I was content to be at home and help John on the farm and do the books for the ranch. Now that I am home more I got used to John and John Sr. dropping in for a morning cup of coffee and to cool off from the morning sun. This is where they would plan out what needed to be done for the rest of the day. This was such a regular occurrence that if they didn't come in I would think something has happened in the fields and worry until they did break and come in and I was full of nothing questions. They would be surprised and asked why you are asking so many questions. I would answer didn't you know that farmers have the highest rate of accidents in the United States? Don't you know that I actually care what happens to you in the fields, especially when it's so hot?

I kind of said a while back that I was not well liked by my mother-in-law; it was obvious that she hated me and my mother although she liked my father. Take this story any way you would like to take it and draw your own conclusions about how she felt. My first inclination was the fact that she didn't like the idea of John and I got married. I thought I would be accepted by John's parents as he was by mine. WRONG!!!

There was another time that I went over to my mother-in-laws house to visit with her,(in my mom's home John didn't have to ring the doorbell) we were family, wrong again, Anna was sitting at the table reading the newspaper and she remarked as she got up and went into the den that she was reading and left me alone in the kitchen. There was nothing left for me to do but go home. Remember we live on the same farm and had no neighbors; we lived on opposite corners of the farm.

Still at a later date it was in the hot summer and John had brought sacks of potatoes home and put them in the garage to store them, nothing like good baked potatoes for dinner. I noticed that there were a lot of bugs coming out of the sacks; my first instinct was to spray the sacks. No wait I must ask my mother-in-law if this action of spraying the sacks would soak into the potato. I called and asked what I thought was a good question and received this response, I have never seen a cockroach until your mother served them at the wedding. I got very upset with her and called her a dammed old Nazi and I knew she could have picked a better wife for John that he could for himself. I slammed down the phone and pouted and cried for awhile and I still had no answer for the bugs. All of a sudden my door swung open and John Sr. came into the room yelling did you call Anna a Nazi? I said yes and he was getting redder in the face by the minute, I said don't you want know what she said to me? OK what? I proceeded in telling him and as he said oh no I knew he had heard this many times before. Now here I sat after all these years of marriage and three children did I really realize that I wasn't loved and accepted into this family. If John had not taken my side in this situation I would have felt that this was the time to leave. No after all I married John not his family. John has always remained by my side.

They say time heals all wounds as you read this you know they can be buried, but not forgotten or forgiven. As time went on John's brother and sister married and moved on leaving John home on the farm, which was fine as they each had their lives and children. One of the things that rubbed me the wrong way is the fact that my three boys had to work on the farm; I can't imagine that they would have had enough fight in them to refuse to help. What I am getting at is the boys did the work to help produce the crop, their grandpa would give them part of the profit for their labor, on the other hand all of the cousins received the same amount of it in cash and they never stepped on the field. The only thing that made up for it was that they earned their share by their own hands and labor and they loved their grandpa deeply.

Linda would come home bringing the girls and Anna would take them all shopping for their school wardrobe. Before they would leave to go back to Arizona, Anna and John would take us all out to dinner and then home for desert. One time when Fred, Donna and the kids came home, Linda was there also, Anna called and said they were going to dinner and we could come over for dessert, if we would like to visit the rest of the family. I told John if I am not good enough for dinner then I am not good enough for dessert, therefore your mother can go to hell. He replied I understand and we stayed at home, the next day John Sr. asked why we didn't come over. John told his dad why that day. From that day on John Sr. always told me it made him proud to have me for a daughter-in-law. When we went to the Elk dances he always made sure to dance with me and repeat how proud he was of me. At least he tried to make amends and today I still really love that man.

While dad was sick I would go to the hospital and make sure he was eating, this was his last stint in the hospital, and he never got to come home. One night I went to make sure he could see the football game. They had it on for him and he had made a bet with the other patient in his room and was really enjoying the game. The next morning he was gone, Anna left his room saying at last I am a wealthy woman. All the years that were in the past she kept telling me that she owned the ranch not John Jr. I knew this and I never tried to act otherwise. I guess they all seemed to think I married John for his money. Remember what John owned it was his car. Remember I didn't want to marry a dam farmer. It was not too long ago that Linda, John's sister told me she didn't know why her mother told her she couldn't love or even like me. She said I don't know why? Linda it's because I am of the oaki generation, she felt it was beneath her to have me in her family. I happen to love and respect the heritage that has been given me. It taught me so many things and one of them being not to worship money, money is a tool to be used to sustain the family and its well being, this includes us all. Well let's move on, through all of this I never stopped painting.

In 1985 my parents had both passed and I used my inheritance to put a down payment on our new home. What brought this on was the fact that the kids, wives and girlfriends came to the ranch to visit while they were working, one day I had the house really cleaned up as our attorney was going to pick us up as we had to give deposition in another town and he wanted to talk to us on the way. Well we went to Lancaster, CA. for the deposition and when we arrived home John went in first, turning right around coming back saying you don't want to go in there. I responded with get your ass in the car we are going house shopping. Later that week I bought a lot and picked the floor plan I wanted and put a downpayment on it. It's funny as I told no one, I guess John did, John's father came over and said I hear you are leaving the ranch, yes I answered, a little pause, and John Sr. said is John going with you? He has the option I answered. Then I explained what had happened and I needed some of my own space. Then it dawned on me now I have a house I can call my own. It felt so good to not be beholden to the Slikker family any more.

After awhile we decided to sell the mobile home in Bodfish, CA. John decided he would like to be able to experience the changing of the seasons. At this point we borrowed money from Uncle Kampe for a lot on the mountain up next to the ski lodge. After we sold the mobile home and received the cash we hired a builder to design us a mountain cabin which was to be our retirement home, so everything we ever wanted was built into this home. A mountain home to die for. This was the place where it snowed every winter, it had a lodge and a place to go dancing, oh so romantic, we discovered the elderberries my mother and father loved coming up and I can still see my mom making those elderberry pies. I said hey mom let's have a piece of pie, ok sounds good, got down the plates and a knife for cutting and started to serve, wait I can't cut the crust, mom I can't cut the crust, mom saying you baby don't have any strength huh. She tried and we all had the biggest laugh no one could cut the crust, what did you put in this! cement? When we would go to the dance mom would always fall in love with the drummer and daddy loved to dance with all the ladies. It was a wonderful time for me.

We decided to invest our income from the property that we had invested in a few years earlier. We had a lease for $25,000 per year and we used this money to buy a lot on the coast in Cayucos, Ca. We used the same builder from the mountain home and had him design a tri-plex for us here in Cayucos. The people got a kick out of Ron's business card The Do Da Construction Co. It had a picture of him and his dog in a wheelbarrow being portrayed as mountain people. His dog was always with him on the construction site. We made sure we had a place for each of our parents to stay if they wanted to. John's parents never came and stayed and my parents always brought their mobile home and parked in the parking lot. At this point I just realized that John had furnished me a home every place I had vacationed with my family. All the while I just keep painting on my own using all the information I had learned along the way.

I stayed a lot in Cayucos and started painting with much more gusto, joining the Cayucos art council, here I met the entire cast of artists in the area, I being the only newcomer. I felt that my work was in the same realm as the rest of the work that I saw. Some better and some worse. I helped with the art receptions brought homemade goods for them to all devourer and waited along with the rest of the artist to see who placed and could conceivability place and possibly make a sale. To no avail did this happen. I took note of the winners and vowed to be able to learn more and surpass the winners next month at the show, to no avail did this happen, for the second time I lost to the same winners. Ok the next month it was the same thing. I realized what it was they needed was a worker bee not an artist as it was set in stone that there was no room for another artist in the community.

I later started with the Morro Bay Art Association, here I found it to be the same story, and only the established artist of the community were placing and selling their work. This so intimidated me to the point I was afraid to show my work on the coast. I just went ahead and painted at home on the kitchen table and turned to my greatest ability, my ability to sew. I hung a sign and advertised in the paper and talked to some stores and here I go, I thought I was doing quite well as a seamstress earning between $2,000-$3,000 per month in business. Later I started working at Sears Dept. Stores in the clothing dept. and it wasn't long before I was shifted to the sewing machines, it seemed that they had no one who could demonstrate and sell the expensive machines, being a seamstress I felt right at home. John was spending more time at the coast, he worked and made our place a show place, we hung his sign as president of the piss and moan club. Also we hung his shingle, Asshole's garage.

Let's go back a little in time. John's father had to retire because of his health, John took over the farm and we leased it by the month and John's dad got a take of the profit from the crop. If the market was good he got more or if it was marginal or lost money dad would step aside allowing John to have enough money for the next crop through harvest. This went on for a few years until we lost our loving dad, in his will he gave Fred and Linda each $25,000 dollars John was to inherit the 60 acres that dad had built the house on, having knowing this we invested in a hay barn and built an office and Citrus packing plant on our 60 acres. Well when John's mother came on board, she claimed that dad didn't have the right to do this transaction as it was community property. All in all Fred and Linda received their inheritance and John lost his. During this time period she wanted John to buy the ranch and she sold it to us for $450,000 wanting $50,000 down in cash. I had been putting money away and we gave her what she wanted. During her capacity as executor of the will she told the attorney she did not sell the farm to John and did not receive cash in the amount of $50,000. John at this time in his life loved and believed her when she said no forget the receipt, he too liked the idea of no receipt now there would be no record of his hidden $50,000. When you try to deceive it will come back to bite you in the ass. During this time she told the attorneys that all she wanted was the ability to buy a blouse once in awhile. This woman would go to any lengths to keep the farm out of this oaki's hands.

Things continued on for awhile at least three or four more years and I tried like hell to get along with my mother-in-law as she was all John had left. My parents were already gone and we were in our new home on Highland Knolls. While we were farming we continued with the monthly rent for the land. We were now processing citrus fruit for other growers we had our first terrible freeze, it was so hard and it was affecting farming across the nation. We had a phone call from Al Roker wanting to interview John about the effect of the weather on the citrus fruit. The interview took place at four in the morning here in the west; they showed my son David with the orange in his hand with an ice icicle hanging from the orange and the leaves on the trees. We managed to survive this first freeze and obtain financing for the coming year. As we got on our feet I kept wondering what happened to all that farm aid the people claim that we get when we lose everything for the last year. HELP!!!! I can't believe the general public really thinks farmers get a hand out; we don't even get a hand up. I want to share with you from many years ago.

As farmers and ranchers, dear God, give us the patience and wisdom to understand why a pound of steak at $1.80 is "high" but a 3-once cocktail at $1.50 is acceptable.

And Lord, help me to understand why $3.00 for a ticket to a movie is "not bad", but a $3.50 for a bushel of wheat that makes 50 loaves of bread is considered unreasonable.

And a 50-cent cola at the ball game is OK, but a 20-cent glass of milk for breakfast is inflationary.

Cotton is "too high" at 65 cents a pound, but a $20 shirt is viewed as a bargain. And corn is "too steep" at 3 cents worth in a box of flakes, but the flakes are sold for 50 cents a serving. And also, Lord, help me understand why I have to give an easement to the gas co. so they can cross my property with their gas lines, and before they get it installed the price of gas has doubled.

And while you're at it, dear God, please help me understand the consumer who drives by my field and raises his eyebrows when he sees me driving a $30,000 tractor that he helped put together so he could make money and drive down that right- of-way they took from me to build a road on so he could go hunting and skiing.

Thank you, God, for your past guidance. I hope you can help me make some sense out of all this. And please, God, send some rain.

This prayer was published in Ann Landers Column on Aug.24, 1980. The prices are different but the message is the same. **GOD HAS SENT US DONALD TRUMP IN THE YEAR OF 2016 TO TRY TO HELP US WITH HIS BLESSINGS IN TRYING TO HELP US CHANGE THE COURSE OF THE LOSS OF OUR FARMERS AND FUTURE FARMERS.** I am the wife of one of the most talented farmers that America has ever had and all of the things in the prayer led us to early retirement.

All of the things mentioned about our Donald Trump are on the bad side of the Democrats. President Trump has done everything he can to help all of us in some type of business; he has put our citizens back to work and helped to take them off of welfare. Our Jobless rate is at the lowest point in decades. President Trump we love you. I can still laugh at my grandpa he said you must vote democrat, because this is a democratic country, Uncle Billy said grandpa always voted as a republican, I can still see him laughing with his toothless grin.

ANN LANDERS

Dear Ann Landers I was interested in the letter from the woman whose husband works 12 hours a day, six day a week. She was worried that he might die of a heart attack.

My husband is a farmer. He works 16 hours a day, seven days a week, 365 days a year. I work with him as much as I can. My husband doesn't smoke or drink, and I am not worried about him dying of a heart attack, he MIGHT die from a broken heart.

Our farm is worth about $200,000 but we have less to live on than most people on welfare. Many farmers (including my husband) work for less than the minimum wage. When one considers the hours he puts in and how important weather can be to his entire crop, it's a shame.

Did you know that farmers represent only four per cent of the population? At one time more than 30 percent of Americans lived on farms.

We have no political influence. People who know nothing about farming make the laws that regulate our lives. We are being squeezed out of existence. No young person in his right mind wants to make farming his life's work. And who can blame him? If young people refuse to farm, who is going to feed this nation? Sign me--- worried sick in Bakersfield, CA. This was written at the time Bob Bergland was Secretary of Agriculture. I am also the wife of a farmer John Slikker and these same people over the years have regulated the farmer and farms that it makes it almost impossible today to make a living, so I say **THANK YOU DONALD TRUMP FOR ALL THE THINGS YOU ARE DOING, THE THINGS TO MAKE AMERICA STRONG AND GREAT AGAIN!!!!** We managed to get the bank to loan us money for the farm for one year. We had to show a plan and a production report for the year, including all of the expenses and the projected gross profit. Let's not worry about the net profit, it was simple the bank came first and then we lived on the left over profit, sometimes good and sometimes not so good, but we made due. After a few years John lost his mother and all hell broke loose again with Fred and Linda wanting us to buy the ranch as the attorneys had nullified the earlier transaction between John and his mother. At this time we considered letting them sell the Ranch to strangers (which is what we should have done) but our sons wanted so much to continue with grandpa's farm that we gave in and made the purchase of $450,000 (what happened to my $50,000) oh I remember

Anna convinced everyone that we didn't pay that money to her in the first transaction. Fluked again!!!

Another great surprise, John's mother declared that John had predeceased him leaving no spouse or children. This seemed to please both Linda and Fred. Oh my god Fred gets nothing if Linda lives on for another 30 days. It was at this point that Fred decided it wasn't fair to John so he helped his brother get through all of this. Having being raised the way I was I couldn't keep my nose out of their business, I made John give up his grudge against both Fred and Linda. For awhile Fred and John did a lot of things together, then came our 50th wedding anniversary, we invited Fred and Linda (which would be their first meeting since the trouble began). We spent time with them both and I guess Fred didn't like it and hasn't spoken to John since, Linda on the other hand talks to John all the time.

Life goes on and we are in the citrus packing business and growing hay that we sold to our horse customers and we had the title of "SLIKKER HAY CO." I sold hay from the ranch to our regular customers and we delivered hay to out of town. We got the reputation for having the best hay that could be found and was commissioned to produce hay for Universal Studio animals. The fellows really enjoyed that trip, and then we had to go to the farm that had the animals for movies. Only the best would do. On the weekends I would continue to paint mostly on my own. I think we managed to get going on the farm until late 1996, another freeze just as we were getting our feet on the ground. This freeze was by far the worst destructive to the Slikker organization than any we had endured. At this point I must go back to 1985, we built the triplex and in a few years we sold it and invested in a farm in Arvin, California area, a fantastic piece of land with the best soil you could grow and type of crop. After putting a lot of money into it we sold the property to pay off the bank and try to get out of debt. Unfortunately this did not happen and a few years later we had to sell grandpa's farm, this the kids did not take lightly, but it had to go. We then got a loan to keep the few acres that had our home and packing shed to the tune of $400,000. This meant we needed to procure growers that we could pack and ship their fruit; everything is set in motion at the time. Coming later was the biggest freeze in our history. More phone calls from Al Roker in NYC wanting to know how this was going to affect the crops again. This time the story was different the growers lost everything, ah yes the government was going to help the growers out this time and all the workers that lost their jobs. There would be no harvest this year. How do I make the payments on the $400,000 loan against the property? Yes I'll file for the disaster loan also just enough to cover the expenses until next year's harvest. Wrong I was no longer a farmer (formally) I was now considered to be a packer. I can't say that word again, in 1997 John and I filed for Bankruptcy losing everything we had worked for. We got to keep the house at the beach simply because we had it homesteaded. This house was purchased in 1986 after my father Bill Shultz had passed away. After the freeze had wiped us out I moved to the house at the beach and we put a trailer under the hay barn, we would stay there during the week and come home on weekend until all this happened to us. It was during this period that a black cat, we called him hobo, came to the packing shed. It took us awhile to get him to take up with us. We would leave him in the packing shed over the weekend and let him stay with us in the trailer during the week. John soon let me adopt him and bring him home to stay at the house. He gave us a lot of comfort while we were going through our hard times. Remember I said that if things ever got really hard for us I could still make it through, I did but it was a hard job to drag John along. He found work with another packing house and helped them and ran their crew. I stayed in Cayucos and got my job at Sears. I think I told you about that already. While we were there I kept telling John that we needed to sell the house and find a place we could afford to make the payments. Our payment was $2,000 a month on this house. It was beautiful and I would hate to leave. On one of our trips, by train to Reno, Nevada, I was talking about finding another place that we could afford. We needed enough to pay off the loan on this house and buy another one with enough money left over to retire on. On this trip John turned and said we need to sell our house and move to Nevada, the thought of living in Nevada pleased him and he could play and see shows at will. We sat about conquering this feat; John had me looking on the computer for affordable places to live. We found **PAHRUMP!!!!**

Ok let's see where I go from here, how shall I make myself known in the art world of Pahrump. While we were building our home we had to get carpet and tile from a certain store. They had the contract with our builder and while I was in the store, I mentioned that I was an artist and I needed a floor that would hold up in case I messed it up with my paints and brushes. He started giving me some samples and suggestions all the time he kept coming back to my art. He asked if I had any pictures of the type of thing that I do, showed him pictures just as you would of your child, being proud of what I was doing. He said Dang would you like to do a promotion for us? I asked what he meant by promotion, he said when a customer buys x amount of carpet from us we let them pick one of your paintings for their new home. The more they upgrade the more we will pay you for your painting starting at $100.00 each. That month they sold 10 paintings, I earned $1000.00 that was not bad after all the stops had been thrown in my path the last few years.

Another store saw my work and said you should be showing at the court house, how I do that, I replied and he gave me the phone number that I should call and I went home and did just that. A kind old gentleman answered the phone and I told him what I wanted to do, sure he replied be here at the court house and bring three pieces of your work and we will hang them along with the rest of the group. I did just that. Two women came up to me and introduced themselves to me and asked what I wanted to accomplish in Pahrump in the field of art. I answered with to be as busy as I can be and show and sell my art and pursue an artistic reputation so I can gain recognition for my work. These ladies put me right to work in different committees no more free time on my hands. During my first year in Pac I heard about the art show ART & SOL, this was a show for crafters and artist to show and sell the work in a formal park art show, this I had never done before. I had a student (a child) and told her if she wanted to be in my booth to sell some of her work she was more than welcome, just be sure to be on time and expect to be busy selling your work, you cannot go off and play and expect me to sell your work, your relatives and friends will want to purchase from you direct. It was very successful for her as her family and family friends came and really supported her she had very little left over to sell. I on the other hand had the same problems as I always had, more to take home. I was so pleased for Rachel.

A lady came up to my booth and asked for a painting for the silent auction, I was more than happy to oblige her and let her pick the one they wanted in the auction. I went over to the auction booth to watch and see how this went on. This lady was in charge and her name is Doris Smith, she remarked we are going to be the best of friends, I ask why and she replied we paint alike. Her work was gorgeous and I was pleased to have met Doris. I have been in Pahrump for 18 years and yes we have been the best of friends. From that show on I was the chairman for the next 5 years. Everyone wondered why they never sold any of their work, having been in marketing the last 13 years, it didn't matter what the product was dresses, hay, art, you have to market yourself. You had to make the public that your product was the best to be seen, and if it was your hay it had to put up just right for the horse trade, you had to convince them that it was, it had to stand up to the quality. The same for art, clients like to feel they have a personal connection to you and that they have purchased this beautiful piece of work from a friend. Doris and I did a few projects together. One weekend we did a private showing that was open to the public with only Doris and I as the only artists in the show. Our friend Jack Sanders owner of Sander's Winery gave us use of his winery

Dorothy Slikker at her private show at the winery

Figure 2 Dorothy Slikker and Doris Smith

We had the most wonderful time that day eating and showing our wares. This is the one friend that can get me into a lot of trouble, she loves to travel all over and paint with the masters. This is the dear friend that got me involved in Las Vegas Painting Convention and painting with the same teachers, she had been showing me the work that she did under her guidance, and boy did I ever want to have the same experience. My first year out I painted with Bill Bayer and Johnnie Lillidahl. Painting with Bill Bayer was a pleasant experience as his method was the same as what I had experienced under other artist. Johnnie Lillidahl was a whole different ball game, when she taught a certain part of the painting she would explain why certain things would be done in a certain way. Such as she told us to paint the face of our girl in this picture the same as the soil colors because the earth would be reflecting upon the face. Putting a curve over the belly part of the female as all women have a curve over the belly and this will help the viewer of this painting to know it's a female.

All this time I kept teaching classes and taking a break for the week while I was at the convention. Lenora Danielson was one of my first adult students; we met when she came to the Busy Bee art school for little ones. I had her grandson in class. Lenora told me she really wanted to learn to paint and she was more than willing to take a seat along with the little ones. I told her I would be glad to have her as a student but she would have to come to my studio to take the classes.

On her first class I asked her Lenora what is it you expect to learn from this class. She explained that she wanted to learn to paint and be creative as she could be was getting ready to retire and needed to have something more in her life to fill it with a challenge. We started in and Lenora stayed with me for about four years. She followed all the steps that I taught her and she learned to turn out some masterpieces. Lenora went on and entered different art shows and fall festivals earning cash money along with high placement ribbons. She and Doris formed a partnership and opened THE DUSTY BURRO art and gift shop in Death Valley Junction. They were quite successful in their venture. Lenora went on and built herself a cabin in the city of Goldfield and has made it her home for her art and gem shop. She has it on hold for awhile as her son Chip is very ill at this time and this takes up a lot of her waking hours. She has taught herself to take pictures and paint some very heartwarming originals. There was one time that I got Lenora to attend the Creative Painting Convention, she felt that she couldn't keep up so for her one time was enough as you look at her paintings you can see she didn't need to take those lessons for what it was that she had set her goals. Learning enough to keep her busy in her retirement year which was what she wanted to learn for.

Lenora was just like Doris, she held down the president's job, in the art group, that Doris helped to start; she also helped to start the art gallery next to the Pahrump library. Lenora's father was of Indian descent and had some rugs and stones, mostly gems and left them to her. She in turn started making jewelry and then painting on old cans and oil cans whatever she could find. Later she even got smart enough to bottle some desert dust and sold Death Valley Soil to the tourist. I feel this woman is a complete genius. If you remember I was a seamstress and I had so many sewing machines, here is Lenora her machine just took a crap, so I gave her one and some quilting stuff and she proceeded to make blankets for her new cabin. She is a wonder woman. Remember when you see her work on the next page, this woman had never held a brush in her hand, see what she was able to accomplish. Lenora had the one thing I said you needed to have to learn to paint, the desire to paint. Congratulations Lenora!!!

Lenora Danielson with her award winning master pieces

Let me now take the time to tell you a little about Doris Smith. I told you how we met and how she paints.

I feel I need you to know that Doris is the artist that has tried very hard to start an organization to help the artist rise above the putdown of the term Pahrump artist. She feels, as I do, that we are a special group, in our own right, and deserve to be held in high esteem as we produce some of the most sought after pieces of art in the state of Nevada. Doris volunteers for most of all the events held in Pahrump that deals with art. She spent many years giving art lessons to the seniors at the senior center, she also holds and has done this for many years, a class for three women who come together and paint, as I would say chew the fat. This is a ritual has been happening for many years. They bring food and eat, paint and tell lies, laugh and have a ball.

The next four Art & Sol's that was chairman of were held in different places; I had them in the Nugget and Sanders winery and managed to raise money for PAC. (Pahrump Art Council) I felt these were places the Artist could shine. We invited artist from Vegas and some came from the area of Palm Springs. I worked hard to raise the bar for the artist but nothing seemed to work they always presented themselves in their own way. At this point I decided that I would work on marketing myself.

I told you that I was going to the Vegas Art Convention and Doris kept having me to try and get to teach at this event. On our second trip there I met Robert Warren and took classes from him, and I observed how he went about teaching. Later Doris and I went to Carson City and painted for a week with Gary Jenkins in his home, after that class, I realized that I could do the same, as they were only human. Therefore I applied and was accepted to teach my golfer. It was during this time that I started fainting and getting short of breath, one day at the Dr's. office as I sat in the waiting room I told his nurse that I couldn't breathe, he told me to wait for a min and then came back, took me into the back and put the meter on my finger, saying my god you can't breathe, that's what I have been saying. The Dr. proceed to order oxygen for me and I was ok for awhile. A few months later we went to a wedding in Bakersfield and I felt sick and we left early, the next day we drove home and went to have something to eat, I got sick and told John we must go now as I don't feel right. We went home and I still couldn't keep anything down getting sick a couple more times and I said we need to go the emergency room. With the symptoms of being sick and the pain they thought I had stones. They kept me in the hospital as they had to remove them in a different way as there was no way I was going to pass them. During the night I had called the nurse to help me to the bathroom, when she got there I had passed out and when I came to the Dr. was slapping my face saying she came back. I guess I was sicker than I thought. The next day the nurse said I had scared them because it seemed that I had died. People have asked me about what it was like and all I could say was it was so peaceful. I knew that from this point on I had now fear of death. I had four surgeries and the last one was done with a robot to reconstruct my kidney and I spent 12 days in intensive care. Well there was no way that I could teach that class in this condition. Doris Smith stepped up to the plate and with John's help they taught the class and everything was fine. The following year I joined the Western Teachers Association. The teachers from all around the Western United States, I entered their art show and took first place with my "I THINK WE GOT ONE GRANDPA" the judges were all of these famous artist such as Robert Warren. I felt this was a great honor. Whenever I sell this painting all of the awards and ribbons will go with it. It proudly hangs above my fireplace so I can enjoy it each and every day.

Robert Warren is the artist that had the certification classes painting in the same method that I wanted to have my work look like. He is the greatest artist I have ever met. I found out from him about his certification class and talked it over with John to see if he would support my desire to take the course.

Award winning Grandpa I think we got one

This reminds me of John and our grandkids, only their fishing was on the pier at the beach. I felt honored to be in the company of such famous and accomplished artists of today and I hope my work will hold its own. John said ok to my taking the certification course and it took a period of three years. I am now loaded with all of this knowledge so I must keep teaching. The following year I signed up to teach my wolf "On Guard" I had a class of 34 and got great reviews about my method of teaching the class. Doris was my room helper and John sold brushes and extra canvases. I had to get them all through the project in six hours.

On Guard

In order to do this I had to prep the canvas and draw them on each canvas. There were a total of 34 students to prepare for. It was well worth the effort as it made me feel so satisfied. John has really been my rock to be able to fall back on.

I kept entering art contest and not getting anywhere and in the middle of all this the Agora Gallery in NYC notified me for the second time to see if I would like to show in the gallery, if I did would I send pictures and the art critic would pass the judgment whether they passed the quality test for the Agora Gallery. I was notified that I made it into the show to be held in November. I was so pleased, I couldn't swallow my pride and I wanted to shout SOMEBODY WANTS TO SHOW MY WORK my feet never hit the ground for months. Jon my son and his wife Monica took me to NYC for the show; while I was there I visited many more galleries. The Amsterdam Whitney gallery called and asks me to show in their gallery next year.

Meanwhile I kept entering different art magazines for the spot in their magazines. First I made it into the TOP 60 INTERNATIONAL CONTEMPORARY MASTERS. Vivianna made me so proud and I had interviews with her through Skype, I felt that I was on top of the world.

Next came my acceptance with the TOP 100 WORLD CONTEMPORARY MASTERS, again I couldn't control my emotions, now I followed with the Masters in England when they had shows my work was being shown virtually all over the world. I was ecstatic when I was able to show with the top 100 contemporary masters in Las Vegas.

Thank you Tom and Despina Tunberg, for the show of my life, at the Metropolitan Gallery Las Vegas Art Museum, after this show the museum kept two of my pieces.

Dorothy and Despina Tunberg art curator

After this show the museum kept two of my pieces and the next picture shows how proud I am to have my name among the top 100 worldwide contemporary masters.

Dorothy's name on the roster proud as a button

The following paintings are the ones that the art museum kept for their own collection.

Central Park NYC

I hope they keep these and that many people get to look at and appreciate my art in the future. These are the events in my simple life that let up to making me want to share my work and life with the world. I lived through all the disappointments of being denied the opportunity to pursue my art and then all of the criticism from family and friends and yes even the laughter. I just kept my granny in my heart and forged on using her sayings as the backbone of my life. I am pleased to have had a wonderful husband that stood by my side even when things didn't go in the right direction. John Slikker I am proud that you made me your wife and friend for life, we have been together for 59 years and they have been filled with a lot of disappointments and joy and the road has been an exciting one.

Today the world is facing the immigrant problem, John's family were all immigrants. John's grandfather Cornelius came to the United States of America in the early 1900's and found a place to live and work, in other words get his life in a new world in order and then proceeded to bring his bride Elizabeth DeGus to be with him and have their family in a new country.

Cornelus Slikker

Elizabeth DeGus

These are pictures of John's grandparents when they migrated into the USA through Ellis Island in the early 1900's. Elizabeth gave birth to two girls and two boys. There was Cora, John, Bill and Marie. Grandpa started a dairy and the boys worked with him and the girls were being prepared to become housewives and mothers. They stayed in the home learning to take care of their men as they worked on the dairy. This practice seemed to follow the road John took his own path.

Cora, John, Bill and Marie Slikker

Left to right Aunt Cora married a dairyman and had two boys, Ray and Cornelius Veldhouse, John W. Slikker became a farmer and had three children John Jr., Fred and Linda, and Bill Slikker had three children, Diane, Sherri, and Bill Jr. Marie Slikker married a farmer and gave birth to three children, Betty Ann, Janice, and Stanley, as Stanley grew up on the farm the same way John Jr. did he also stayed with the farming industry.

John met and married Anna Marie Seybold, she was from Germany, and her Uncle Fred Kampe brought her to America just before the war broke out in Europe, her mother and father had died from the flu epidemic that went around the world. Anna's sister could not handle the Hitler regime before would 11 was started and had a mental breakdown and had to be hospitalized and she spent her life in that hospital. Taunta and Uncle raised her as if she was their own.

John and Anna Slikker

John and Anna married in the late 1930's and John Jr. was born 6/23/1939. John was working on the dairy with their father in Bakersfield along with his brother Bill, as these boys started raising their own families they left the dairy one at a time and went to work in different fields of labor. The boys had to get different types of work to help with the dairy income.

John working at Golden Crust Bakery and Bill at the oil refinery, life went on as usual for the Slikker family. Anna worked for a short time as a telephone operator and as she started her family she became a full time mother and took care of house and home.

This is a photo of one of our family Christmas's John's dad has opened a package that his mom gave to his dad and she had wrapped a shirt he had never worn, saying she wanted him to have a lot of packages under the tree.

Taunta and Uncle Fred Kampe

They never missed a Christmas at our house; they were always there for the holidays. Taunta and Uncle are the ones of this family that seemed to really love me, they always treated me special.

John's life went on as normal with him participating in his school activities and visiting with friends and relatives during the holiday's and learning to work on the farm. When he worked for his father he was paid and therefore he could pay for his dates and eventually he saved enough to buy his own car. John got to order his brand new 1957 Chevrolet Bel Air HardTop; it was turquoise and light tan or cream in color. He promptly put a truck horn in the trunk and cut outs on the sides of the car, right up town and real sporty. We drove the car for nearly 10 years and traded it in for a Ford Fairlane, a car a little newer and more reliable for our young family. John spent his high school years running around with his group of Edison buddies, they liked to fish and drink. They had John with them at all times and when they drank too much John drove them home. They had him doing this even though he was not old enough to have a driver's license. John was in hog heaven. John would even drive them to the coast so they could go out In the boat fishing. After I met John and he introduced me to Sonny I never liked him as he always talked about how he went and took John out and got him bread. This was all in fun as Sonny was one of John's best friends and he was a groom's man in our wedding. John was a well rounded farm boy and I a farm girl, we felt that our lives would mesh well as we both had the knowledge of what to expect out of a marriage and it did help to be marrying your best friend. A friendship we developed as we kept putting each other first. I had a friend that was on her third marriage ask me how do you do it. How can you stay married to one man for so long? I told her I married my best friend and I love him deeply, we like and do the same thing and we stand by each other and have our hand out at all times just in case we need to touch and hold onto each other. We never place blame on one of us if things failed because we made that decision together.

ALL AND ALL OUR BOND IS STRONG AND FILLED WITH LOVE. John I love you and cherish the time we have had on this earth together.

www.ingramcontent.com/pod-product-compliance
Lightning Source LLC
LaVergne TN
LVHW011738060526
838200LV00051B/3233